Biblical Bravery

Joshua Rhoades

Published by Joshua Paul Rhoades, 2024.

While every precaution has been taken in the preparation of this book, the publisher assumes no responsibility for errors or omissions, or for damages resulting from the use of the information contained herein.

BIBLICAL BRAVERY

First edition. August 27, 2024.

ISBN: 979-8227562760

Written by Joshua Rhoades.

Also by Joshua Rhoades

Courage Under Fire: David's Stand On The Battlefield
Jonah's Journey: Voices Of Redemption And Lessons In Obedience
The Furnace Of Faith: 12 Principles From The Heat Of Faith
Whispers of Hope: Inspiring Stories of Men's Prayers In Scripture
Frontier Legends: The Oregon Dream
Elijah: A Beacon Of Boldness
HOOK, LINE & SAVIOUR - Faith Reflections from Fishing
Driven By Faith: Motor Racing Inspired Christian Life
30 Day Devotional - Bold and Strong- Coffee Devotions for a Courageous Christian Walk
Authentic Christianity: The Heart of Old Time Religion
Consider The Ant - God's Tiny Preachers
Flee Fornication: The Plea For Purity
Renewed Hope- How to Find Encouragement in God
Sounding The Call - The Voice of Conviction
The Altar - Where Heaven Meets Earth
The Bible's Battlefields- Timeless Lessons from Ancient Wars
The Sacred Art of Silence - How Silence Speaks in Scripture
Under Fire- The Sanctity of the Traditional Biblical Home
Who Is on the Lord's Side? A Call to Righteousness
What Is Truth? - From Skepticism to Submission

First and Goal- Faith and Football Fundamentals
From Dugout to Devotion- Spiritual Lessons from Baseball
Par for the Course- Faith and Fairways
The Believer's Pace- Tools for Running Life's Marathon
The Immutable Fortress- Security in God's Unchanging Nature
Biblical Bravery

Introduction

Biblical bravery is a multifaceted concept rooted in the teachings and narratives of the Bible, characterized by unwavering faith, moral integrity, and the courage to act according to divine principles despite facing adversity, danger, or societal opposition. It is a form of courage that transcends mere physical valor, encompassing spiritual resilience, ethical steadfastness, and a deep-seated trust in God's plan. This kind of bravery is exemplified through various biblical figures whose lives and actions serve as timeless lessons for believers. Understanding biblical bravery involves delving into its defining elements, historical examples, and its critical relevance in contemporary society.

At its core, biblical bravery is grounded in faith. It is the courage that arises from a profound belief in God's presence, power, and promises. This faith-driven bravery compels individuals to stand firm in their convictions, even when faced with overwhelming challenges or threats. The Bible presents numerous instances where faith underpins acts of bravery, highlighting the importance of relying on divine strength rather than human capability. For example, David's confrontation with Goliath was not merely a display of physical courage but an act of faith in God's deliverance. David's declaration, "The Lord who rescued me from the paw of the lion and the paw of the bear will rescue me from the hand of this Philistine" (1 Samuel 17:37), underscores that his bravery was rooted in trust in God's protection.

Another critical aspect of biblical bravery is moral integrity. It involves the steadfast adherence to ethical principles and divine commands, even when such adherence entails significant personal risk or sacrifice. Joseph's resistance to Potiphar's wife, as recounted in Genesis 39, exemplifies this aspect of biblical bravery. Despite persistent temptation and the threat of false accusation, Joseph chose to uphold his integrity, declaring, "How then can I do this great wickedness, and sin against God?" (Genesis 39:9). His bravery was demonstrated in his unwavering commitment to righteousness, even at the cost of his freedom.

Biblical bravery also entails a readiness to act in the face of danger or uncertainty, driven by a sense of divine mission. This readiness is evident in the story of Esther, who risked her life to plead for her people's salvation. Her famous words, "If I perish, I perish" (Esther 4:16), reflect a courageous willingness to sacrifice her safety for a higher cause. Esther's bravery was not just about confronting a physical threat but about fulfilling a divine purpose, underscoring the intersection of courage and divine calling.

The narratives of the Bible provide numerous examples of individuals who embodied these aspects of bravery, offering timeless lessons for believers. Daniel's unwavering prayer life, even when threatened with the lions' den, illustrates the bravery of spiritual steadfastness. His continued devotion, despite the decree that praying to anyone other than the king would result in death, demonstrates his courageous commitment to his faith. Similarly, Shadrach, Meshach, and Abednego's refusal to worship the golden image, even under the threat of being thrown into a fiery furnace, exemplifies the bravery of maintaining one's convictions in the face of deadly consequences.

In the New Testament, the apostles' bold proclamation of the gospel, despite persecution, exemplifies the bravery of mission-driven action. The apostle Paul's numerous missionary journeys, filled with hardships, beatings, and imprisonments, highlight his relentless courage in spreading the message of Christ. His declaration, "I can do all things through Christ which strengtheneth me" (Philippians 4:13), encapsulates the essence of biblical bravery – a reliance on divine strength to fulfill God's calling, regardless of the obstacles.

The need for biblical bravery today is more pressing than ever. In an increasingly complex and often hostile world, believers are confronted with numerous challenges that test their faith, integrity, and willingness to stand for what is right. The societal pressures to conform to secular norms, the erosion of moral values, and the prevalence of injustice and persecution make the call for biblical bravery urgent.

One of the most significant challenges facing believers today is the pressure to conform to secular norms that often contradict biblical teachings. In many societies, the biblical worldview on issues such as marriage, sexuality, and sanctity of life is increasingly marginalized. Believers who uphold these principles may face ridicule, discrimination, or even legal consequences. Biblical bravery is needed to stand firm in these convictions, not out of a desire to impose beliefs on others, but out of a commitment to living authentically according to God's Word. This bravery is exemplified by modern-day figures who have faced significant backlash for their faith-based stances, yet remain unwavering in their commitment to biblical truth.

The erosion of moral values in contemporary society further underscores the need for biblical bravery. In a world where ethical relativism often prevails, standing up for absolute moral truths requires courage. This bravery is not about being confrontational but about living out one's faith with integrity and consistency. It involves making ethical decisions that align with biblical principles, even when such decisions are unpopular or countercultural. For instance, in the business world, this might mean refusing to engage in dishonest practices or exploitation, despite potential financial loss or professional repercussions.

Moreover, the prevalence of injustice and persecution in various parts of the world demands a response of biblical bravery. In many countries, Christians face severe persecution for their faith, including imprisonment, violence, and even death. The bravery of these believers, who continue to practice their faith despite such threats, is a powerful testament to the enduring relevance of biblical bravery. Their stories inspire others to stand firm in their faith and to advocate for religious freedom and justice.

Biblical bravery also plays a crucial role in addressing social injustices and advocating for the marginalized and oppressed. The biblical mandate to "seek justice, love mercy, and walk humbly with your God" (Micah 6:8) calls believers to act bravely in the face of injustice. This includes standing against racism, inequality, and oppression, and working towards a society that reflects the values of God's kingdom. The bravery required to confront systemic injustice often involves personal sacrifice, risk, and the willingness to challenge powerful interests. However, it is rooted in the biblical conviction that all people are created in the image of God and deserving of dignity and justice.

Furthermore, the rapid pace of technological and cultural change in the modern world presents unique challenges that require biblical bravery. The digital age has brought about unprecedented access to information and communication, but it has also given rise to issues such as cyberbullying, online harassment, and the spread of misinformation. Believers are called to navigate this landscape with discernment and courage, upholding truth and integrity in their online interactions. This includes bravely speaking out against falsehoods, promoting positive and constructive dialogue, and using digital platforms to share the gospel and advocate for biblical values.

In personal relationships and everyday interactions, biblical bravery manifests as the courage to love and forgive, to seek reconciliation, and to stand by one's principles. It involves being a witness to the transformative power of the gospel through actions and words, even when it is difficult or uncomfortable. This kind of bravery is evident in the willingness to extend grace and forgiveness to those who have wronged us, reflecting the love of Christ in our interactions with others.

The church, as a community of believers, plays a vital role in fostering and supporting biblical bravery. It provides a space for believers to encourage and strengthen one another, to share stories of courage and faith, and to collectively seek God's guidance and strength. Through worship, teaching, and fellowship, the church equips believers to face the challenges of the world with bravery rooted in faith. It also serves as a witness to the broader society, demonstrating the power of a community united by a shared commitment to God's principles.

In conclusion, biblical bravery is a dynamic and multifaceted concept that involves unwavering faith, moral integrity, and the courage to act according to divine principles. It is exemplified by numerous figures in the Bible who faced immense challenges with steadfastness and trust in God. The need for such bravery is more pressing than ever in today's complex and often hostile world. Believers are called to stand firm in their convictions, to uphold moral values, to advocate for justice, and to navigate the challenges of the modern world with discernment and courage. Biblical bravery is not just about grand heroic acts but also about the everyday choices and actions that reflect a commitment to God's truth and love. As believers embrace this call to bravery, they can draw strength from the examples of those who have gone before them and from the assurance of God's presence and guidance in their lives.

Chapter 1 - Strength of Biblical Bravery

"And David said to Saul, Let no man's heart fail because of him; thy servant will go and fight with this Philistine." (1 Samuel 17:32)

In the Bible, one of the most powerful stories of bravery is the story of David facing Goliath. David, a young shepherd boy, displayed incredible strength and courage when he stepped forward to fight Goliath, a giant Philistine warrior who had been terrorizing the Israelite army. The story begins with the Philistines and the Israelites preparing for battle. The Philistines had a champion named Goliath, who was over nine feet tall and wore a coat of armor that weighed around 125 pounds. Goliath stood and shouted to the ranks of Israel, challenging them to send out a champion to fight him one-on-one, saying that if he won, the Israelites would become their servants, but if the Israelite won, the Philistines would serve Israel. For forty days, Goliath came forward every morning and evening, taunting the Israelites. King Saul and the entire Israelite army were terrified and dismayed because no one dared to face Goliath. David, the youngest son of Jesse, was sent by his father to the battlefield to bring food to his older brothers who were in Saul's army. When David arrived, he heard Goliath's defiance and saw the fear in the Israelite camp. Unlike the seasoned soldiers, David was not afraid. He was outraged that Goliath would defy the armies of the living God. David asked the men standing near him what would be done for the man who killed Goliath and removed this disgrace from Israel. David's oldest brother, Eliab, heard him speaking with the men and burned with anger at him. He asked David why he had come down and with whom he had left the few sheep in the wilderness. Eliab accused David of being conceited and having a wicked heart. But David replied, "Now what have I done? Can't I even speak?" David then went to King Saul and said, "Let no one lose heart on account of this Philistine; your servant will go and fight him." Saul replied that David was not able to go out against Goliath because he was only a young man, and Goliath had been a warrior from his youth. But David persisted, telling Saul about how he had fought off lions and bears as a shepherd to protect his father's sheep. David said, "The Lord who rescued me from the paw of the lion and the paw of the bear will rescue me from the hand of this Philistine." Saul said to David, "Go, and the Lord be with you." Saul then dressed David in his own tunic, put a coat of armor on him, and a bronze helmet on his head. David fastened on Saul's sword over the tunic and tried walking around, but he was not used to them. "I cannot go in these," he said to Saul, "because I am not used to them." So he took them off. Then David took his staff in his hand, chose five smooth stones from the stream, put them in the pouch of his shepherd's bag, and, with his sling in his hand, approached Goliath. Meanwhile, Goliath, with his shield-bearer in front of him, kept coming closer to David. He looked David over and saw that he was little more than a boy, glowing with health and handsome, and he despised him. He said to David, "Am I a dog, that you come at me with sticks?" And the Philistine cursed David by his gods. "Come here," he said, "and I'll give your flesh to the birds and the wild animals!" David said to the Philistine, "You come against me with sword and spear and javelin, but I come against you in the name of the

Lord Almighty, the God of the armies of Israel, whom you have defied. This day the Lord will deliver you into my hands, and I'll strike you down and cut off your head. This very day I will give the carcasses of the Philistine army to the birds and the wild animals, and the whole world will know that there is a God in Israel. All those gathered here will know that it is not by sword or spear that the Lord saves; for the battle is the Lord's, and he will give all of you into our hands." As the Philistine moved closer to attack him, David ran quickly toward the battle line to meet him. Reaching into his bag and taking out a stone, he slung it and struck the Philistine on the forehead. The stone sank into his forehead, and he fell facedown on the ground. So David triumphed over the Philistine with a sling and a stone; without a sword in his hand, he struck down the Philistine and killed him. David ran and stood over him. He took hold of the Philistine's sword and drew it from the sheath. After he killed him, he cut off his head with the sword. When the Philistines saw that their hero was dead, they turned and ran. Then the men of Israel and Judah surged forward with a shout and pursued the Philistines to the entrance of Gath and to the gates of Ekron. Their dead were strewn along the Shaaraim road to Gath and Ekron. When the Israelites returned from chasing the Philistines, they plundered their camp. David took the Philistine's head and brought it to Jerusalem; he put the Philistine's weapons in his own tent. As Saul watched David going out to meet the Philistine, he said to Abner, commander of the army, "Abner, whose son is that young man?" Abner replied, "As surely as you live, Your Majesty, I don't know." The king said, "Find out whose son this young man is." As soon as David returned from killing the Philistine, Abner took him and brought him before Saul, with David still holding the Philistine's head. "Whose son are you, young man?" Saul asked him. David said, "I am the son of your servant Jesse of Bethlehem." This story of David and Goliath is not just a tale of a boy defeating a giant; it is a powerful demonstration of faith, courage, and the strength that comes from trusting in God. David's bravery was rooted in his unwavering belief that God would deliver him from danger, just as He had in the past. This account encourages believers to have faith in God's power and to face their giants, no matter how insurmountable they may seem, with confidence that God is with them.

Chapter 2 – Steadfastness of Biblical Bravery

"Though he slay me, yet will I trust in him: but I will maintain mine own ways before him." (Job 13:15)

In the Bible, the story of Job is a powerful example of steadfastness and perseverance through trials. Job was a wealthy man who lived in the land of Uz. He was known for his piety, integrity, and his fear of God. Job was blessed with a large family, many servants, and great wealth in the form of livestock. However, Job's faith and steadfastness were put to the ultimate test when Satan challenged God, claiming that Job was only faithful because he was prosperous. God allowed Satan to test Job, but not to harm him physically. In a series of devastating events, Job lost all his possessions, his servants were killed, and all his children died in a great windstorm that collapsed the house where they were feasting. Despite these immense losses, Job did not sin or blame God foolishly. Instead, he mourned deeply, tore his robe, shaved his head, and fell to the ground in worship, saying, "Naked came I out of my mother's womb, and naked shall I return thither: the Lord gave, and the Lord hath taken away; blessed be the name of the Lord" (Job 1:21). This remarkable response highlighted Job's unwavering faith and steadfastness in the face of unimaginable grief. The story did not end there. Satan then challenged God again, arguing that Job would surely curse God if he were to suffer physically. God permitted Satan to afflict Job with painful sores from the soles of his feet to the crown of his head. Job's suffering was so intense that he sat among the ashes, using a broken piece of pottery to scrape his sores. Job's wife, overwhelmed by their losses and seeing her husband's torment, urged him to curse God and die. But Job rebuked her, saying, "Thou speakest as one of the foolish women speaketh. What? shall we receive good at the hand of God, and shall we not receive evil?" (Job 2:10). In all this, Job did not sin with his lips. Job's steadfastness was further tested when his three friends, Eliphaz, Bildad, and Zophar, came to visit him. They sat with him in silence for seven days, mourning his suffering. However, when they finally spoke, they suggested that Job's suffering must be a punishment for some hidden sin. They argued that God is just and would not allow an innocent person to suffer so greatly. Job defended his integrity, insisting that he had not committed any sin that warranted such punishment. He expressed his deep anguish and confusion, but he never lost his faith in God. Job's dialogues with his friends spanned many chapters, during which he maintained his righteousness and steadfastness. One of the most profound declarations of Job's steadfast faith comes in Job 13:15, where he says, "Though he slay me, yet will I trust in him: but I will maintain mine own ways before him." This verse encapsulates Job's unwavering trust in God's sovereignty, even though he did not understand the reasons for his suffering. Job's steadfastness in the face of severe trials and his refusal to curse God exemplify true biblical bravery. Throughout his ordeal, Job yearned for an audience with God to plead his case and understand why he was suffering. Despite his intense pain and the accusations from his friends, Job clung to his faith, believing that God would ultimately vindicate him. Job's perseverance was finally rewarded when God spoke to him out of a whirlwind, questioning him about the mysteries of the universe and the natural world.

Through these questions, God revealed His omnipotence and the limitations of human understanding. Job realized the greatness of God and the futility of questioning His ways. In response, Job humbled himself and repented, saying, "I know that thou canst do every thing, and that no thought can be withholden from thee. Who is he that hideth counsel without knowledge? therefore have I uttered that I understood not; things too wonderful for me, which I knew not. Hear, I beseech thee, and I will speak: I will demand of thee, and declare thou unto me. I have heard of thee by the hearing of the ear: but now mine eye seeth thee. Wherefore I abhor myself, and repent in dust and ashes" (Job 42:2-6). God restored Job's fortunes, giving him twice as much as he had before. His brothers, sisters, and acquaintances came to comfort him, and each gave him a piece of silver and a gold ring. Job's latter days were blessed more than his beginning; he had fourteen thousand sheep, six thousand camels, a thousand yoke of oxen, and a thousand donkeys. He also had seven sons and three daughters, who were known for their beauty. Job lived a long life, seeing his children and their children to the fourth generation. Job's story is a testament to the power of steadfastness and faith in the face of overwhelming trials. His unwavering trust in God, despite his profound suffering and the misunderstandings of his friends, exemplifies the kind of bravery that believers are called to exhibit. Job's perseverance shows that even when we do not understand the reasons behind our suffering, we can trust in God's wisdom and sovereignty. The story of Job encourages believers to remain steadfast in their faith, knowing that God is always in control and that He will ultimately bring about justice and restoration. Job's example teaches us that true bravery is not the absence of fear or suffering but the steadfast commitment to trust in God no matter the circumstances. This story from the Bible, written in the King James Version, remains one of the most powerful illustrations of perseverance, faith, and steadfastness, inspiring believers to hold fast to their faith through all of life's trials.

Chapter 3 – Sacrifice In Biblical Bravery

"And he said, Take now thy son, thine only son Isaac, whom thou lovest... and offer him there for a burnt offering..." (Genesis 22:2)

The story of Abraham's willingness to offer his son Isaac as a sacrifice is one of the most profound examples of bravery and faith in the Bible. This story, found in Genesis 22, is a powerful testament to Abraham's unwavering trust in God, even when faced with an unimaginable request. Abraham had waited many years for a son, and God had finally blessed him and his wife Sarah with Isaac in their old age. Isaac was not just any child; he was the child of promise, through whom God had said He would establish His covenant and bring forth a great nation. Despite this, God tested Abraham's faith by asking him to sacrifice Isaac as a burnt offering. The command came suddenly and with great clarity: "And he said, Take now thy son, thine only son Isaac, whom thou lovest, and get thee into the land of Moriah; and offer him there for a burnt offering upon one of the mountains which I will tell thee of" (Genesis 22:2). Abraham's response to this command is a remarkable display of obedience and faith. Early the next morning, without hesitation, Abraham got up and prepared for the journey. He saddled his donkey and took with him two of his servants and his son Isaac. He also split the wood for the burnt offering and set out for the place God had told him about. This immediate obedience is striking because it shows Abraham's complete trust in God, even when the command seemed to contradict God's earlier promises. On the third day of their journey, Abraham looked up and saw the place in the distance. He said to his servants, "Abide ye here with the ass; and I and the lad will go yonder and worship, and come again to you" (Genesis 22:5). This statement is a powerful expression of Abraham's faith. Despite knowing what he was about to do, he spoke with confidence that both he and Isaac would return. This indicates his belief that God could raise Isaac from the dead if necessary, to fulfill His promises. As Abraham and Isaac walked together, Isaac, carrying the wood for the burnt offering, noticed something was missing. He said, "My father: and he said, Here am I, my son. And he said, Behold the fire and the wood: but where is the lamb for a burnt offering?" (Genesis 22:7). Abraham's response was profound and filled with faith: "My son, God will provide himself a lamb for a burnt offering" (Genesis 22:8). This statement not only reassured Isaac but also reflected Abraham's deep trust in God's provision. When they reached the place God had told him about, Abraham built an altar there and arranged the wood on it. He bound his son Isaac and laid him on the altar, on top of the wood. This moment must have been incredibly difficult for Abraham, yet he continued to demonstrate unwavering obedience. As he reached out his hand and took the knife to slay his son, the angel of the Lord called out to him from heaven, saying, "Abraham, Abraham: and he said, Here am I. And he said, Lay not thine hand upon the lad, neither do thou any thing unto him: for now I know that thou fearest God, seeing thou hast not withheld thy son, thine only son from me" (Genesis 22:11-12). Abraham looked up and saw a ram caught by its horns in a thicket. He went over and took the ram and sacrificed it as a burnt offering instead of his son. Abraham named that place Jehovah-jireh, meaning "The Lord Will Provide," to commemorate God's provision and faithfulness. The angel of the Lord called to Abraham a second time and said, "By myself have I sworn, saith the Lord, for because thou hast done this thing, and hast not withheld thy son, thine only son: that in blessing I will bless thee, and in multiplying I will multiply thy seed as the stars of the heaven, and as the sand which is upon the sea shore; and thy seed shall possess the gate of his enemies; and in thy seed shall all the nations of the earth be blessed; because thou hast obeyed my voice" (Genesis 22:16-18). This passage highlights the tremendous blessings that came as a result of Abraham's faith and obedience. Abraham's willingness to sacrifice Isaac is a powerful example of bravery rooted in faith. It shows that true bravery involves trusting God completely, even when His commands seem incomprehensible or incredibly difficult. Abraham's faith was not blind; it was based on his deep relationship with God and his belief in God's promises. He knew that God is faithful and that He would fulfill His promises, even if it required raising Isaac from the dead. This story also foreshadows the ultimate sacrifice that God would make by offering His own Son, Jesus Christ, as a sacrifice for the sins of the world. Just as Abraham did not withhold his beloved son, God did not withhold His only Son but gave Him up for us all. Jesus' sacrifice on the cross is the ultimate demonstration of God's love and provision for humanity. Abraham's example teaches us that true bravery and sacrifice often involve great personal cost and require a deep trust in God's goodness and faithfulness. It challenges us to consider what we are willing to sacrifice in our own lives in obedience to God's will. Are we willing to give up our most treasured possessions, relationships, or dreams if God asks us to? Abraham's story encourages us to trust God's plan and timing, even when we do not understand it fully. It reminds us that God is always in control and that His ways are higher than our ways. When we face difficult decisions or trials, we can look to Abraham's example and find strength and encouragement to persevere in faith. In conclusion, Abraham's willingness to offer Isaac as a sacrifice is a profound demonstration of biblical bravery. His unwavering faith, obedience, and trust in God, even in the face of an unimaginable command, serve as an inspiration to believers. Abraham's story reminds us that true bravery involves sacrifice and complete trust in God's provision and promises. It challenges us to deepen our faith and to be willing to make sacrifices in our own lives in obedience to God's will. Abraham's example encourages us to trust God's plan, even when it is difficult, and to have confidence that God will provide and fulfill His promises.

Chapter 4 – Submission of Biblical Bravery

"Saying, Father, if thou be willing, remove this cup from me: nevertheless not my will, but thine, be done." (Luke 22:42)

In the Bible, the story of Jesus praying in the Garden of Gethsemane is one of the most profound examples of submission and bravery. This story, found in Luke 22:42, shows Jesus facing the most difficult moment of His earthly life with a deep sense of submission to God's will. On the night before His crucifixion, Jesus went to the Garden of Gethsemane with His disciples. He knew that His time had come and that He would soon face immense suffering and death on the cross. Jesus told His disciples to sit while He went to pray, taking Peter, James, and John with Him a little further. He began to be sorrowful and troubled, saying to them, "My soul is exceeding sorrowful, even unto death: tarry ye here, and watch with me" (Matthew 26:38). Jesus went a little farther, fell on His face, and prayed, "O my Father, if it be possible, let this cup pass from me: nevertheless not as I will, but as thou wilt" (Matthew 26:39). This prayer reveals the deep anguish and dread Jesus felt as He contemplated the suffering He was about to endure. He was fully aware of the physical agony of crucifixion and the spiritual weight of bearing the sins of the world. Despite His distress, Jesus expressed His desire for God's will to be done above His own. After praying, Jesus returned to His disciples and found them sleeping. He said to Peter, "What, could ye not watch with me one hour? Watch and pray, that ye enter not into temptation: the spirit indeed is willing, but the flesh is weak" (Matthew 26:40-41).

Jesus went away a second time and prayed, "O my Father, if this cup may not pass away from me, except I drink it, thy will be done" (Matthew 26:42). This repetition of His prayer shows His ongoing struggle and the depth of His submission. He returned again to find His disciples sleeping, their eyes heavy. Leaving them, He went away and prayed the third time, saying the same words. The intensity of Jesus' prayer in Gethsemane is further highlighted in Luke's account, where it says, "And being in an agony he prayed more earnestly: and his sweat was as it were great drops of blood falling down to the ground" (Luke 22:44). This description underscores the extreme emotional and physical distress Jesus experienced, to the point where His sweat became like drops of blood. This condition, known as hematidrosis, can occur under extreme stress. Despite this immense pressure, Jesus continued to submit Himself to God's will. He understood that His suffering and death were necessary for the redemption of humanity. His willingness to go through with it, despite knowing the cost, exemplifies ultimate bravery and submission. After this intense period of prayer, Jesus returned to His disciples and said, "Sleep on now, and take your rest: behold, the hour is at hand, and the Son of man is betrayed into the hands of sinners" (Matthew 26:45). As He spoke, Judas Iscariot, one of His twelve disciples, arrived with a large crowd armed with swords and clubs, sent by the chief priests and elders of the people. Judas had arranged to betray Jesus by giving a signal: "Whomsoever I shall kiss, that same is he: hold him fast" (Matthew 26:48). He went up to Jesus and said, "Hail, master," and kissed Him. Jesus responded, "Friend, wherefore art thou come?" (Matthew 26:50). The men stepped forward, seized Jesus, and arrested Him. At this moment, one of Jesus' companions drew his sword and struck the servant of the high priest, cutting off his ear. Jesus said to him, "Put up again thy sword into his place: for all they that take the sword shall perish with the sword" (Matthew 26:52). He then touched the servant's ear and healed him, demonstrating His commitment to nonviolence and submission to God's plan. Jesus continued, "Thinkest thou that I cannot now pray to my Father, and he shall presently give me more than twelve legions of angels? But how then shall the scriptures be fulfilled, that thus it must be?" (Matthew 26:53-54). Jesus' words reveal His understanding of the necessity of His arrest and crucifixion for the fulfillment of God's redemptive plan. He willingly submitted to the authorities, even though He had the power to resist. Jesus' arrest in Gethsemane and His subsequent trials, suffering, and crucifixion are the ultimate acts of bravery and submission. Throughout this ordeal, Jesus remained focused on fulfilling God's will, demonstrating His unwavering commitment to the salvation of humanity. His prayer in Gethsemane, "Father, if thou be willing, remove this cup from me: nevertheless not my will, but thine, be done" (Luke 22:42), encapsulates the essence of His submission. Jesus' example in Gethsemane teaches us that true bravery is not the absence of fear or distress but the willingness to submit to God's will, even when it is difficult and painful. It shows that submission to God requires trust in His plan and purpose, even when we do not fully understand it. Jesus' submission was not passive resignation but an active choice to align His will with God's. This submission was motivated by His love for the Father and for humanity. His bravery in facing the cross was rooted in His desire to fulfill His mission of redemption. This story challenges us to consider our own willingness to submit to God's will in our lives. Are we willing to trust God and follow His plan, even when it involves sacrifice and suffering? Jesus' example encourages us to seek God's will in all things and to have the courage to say, "Not my will, but thine be done." Jesus' prayer in Gethsemane also highlights the importance of prayer in the face of trials. In His moment of greatest need, Jesus turned to the Father in prayer, seeking strength and guidance. His example shows us that prayer is a vital source of support and sustenance in difficult times. It is through prayer that we can find the strength to submit to God's will and to face the challenges before us. In conclusion, Jesus' prayer in the Garden of Gethsemane is a powerful demonstration of biblical bravery and submission. His willingness to face the cross, despite the immense suffering it entailed, exemplifies the ultimate act of bravery rooted in submission to God's will. Jesus' example teaches us that true bravery involves trusting God and aligning our will with His, even in the face of great difficulty. It challenges us to seek God's will in our lives and to have the courage to follow it, knowing that God's plan is ultimately for our good and His glory.

Chapter 5 – Sincerity of Biblical Bravery

"And Nathan said to David, Thou art the man. Thus saith the Lord God of Israel, I anointed thee king over Israel..." (2 Samuel 12:7)

In the Bible, the story of Nathan confronting David is an extraordinary example of sincerity and bravery. This story, found in 2 Samuel 12:7, illustrates the courage it takes to speak the truth, especially to someone in a position of great power. David, the king of Israel, had committed a grievous sin by taking Bathsheba, the wife of Uriah, and arranging for Uriah's death in battle to cover up his adultery. Despite his position and his previous closeness to God, David had fallen into serious moral failure. God, however, did not abandon David to his sin. Instead, He sent the prophet Nathan to confront David and bring him to repentance. Nathan's task was daunting, as David was not only the king but also a beloved and powerful leader who had the authority to punish or even kill those who opposed him. Nathan's bravery and sincerity are evident in his approach. He did not directly accuse the king but instead used a parable to illustrate David's wrongdoing. Nathan told David a story about two men in a city: one rich and the other poor. The rich man had a very large number of sheep and cattle, while the poor man had nothing except one little ewe lamb, which he had bought. He raised it, and it grew up with him and his children. It shared his food, drank from his cup, and even slept in his arms; it was like a daughter to him. One day, a traveler came to the rich man, but the rich man refrained from taking one of his own sheep or cattle to prepare a meal for the traveler. Instead, he took the ewe lamb that belonged to the poor man and prepared it for his guest. When David heard this story, he burned with anger against the rich man and said to Nathan, "As the Lord liveth, the man that hath done this thing shall surely die: And he shall restore the lamb fourfold, because he did this thing, and because he had no pity" (2 Samuel 12:5-6). At this critical moment, Nathan demonstrated profound sincerity and bravery by delivering God's message directly. He said to David, "Thou art the man. Thus saith the Lord God of Israel, I anointed thee king over Israel, and I delivered thee out of the hand of Saul; And I gave thee thy master's house, and thy master's wives into thy bosom, and gave thee the house of Israel and of Judah; and if that had been too little, I would moreover have given unto thee such and such things. Wherefore hast thou despised the commandment of the Lord, to do evil in his sight? Thou hast killed Uriah the Hittite with the sword, and hast taken his wife to be thy wife, and hast slain him with the sword of the children of Ammon" (2 Samuel 12:7-9). Nathan's words were a direct indictment of David's sins, highlighting not only the murder of Uriah but also the abuse of his royal power and the betrayal of his divine calling. Nathan's bravery is evident in his willingness to confront the king with such a harsh and unequivocal message. He risked his own safety and position to deliver God's truth, demonstrating that true bravery involves speaking the truth in love, regardless of the potential consequences. Nathan's confrontation had a profound impact on David. Instead of reacting with anger or defensiveness, David was struck with conviction. He acknowledged his sin and said to Nathan, "I have sinned against the Lord" (2 Samuel 12:13). Nathan then assured David of God's mercy, telling him, "The Lord also hath put away thy sin; thou shalt not die. Howbeit, because by this deed thou hast given great occasion to the enemies of the Lord to blaspheme, the child also that is born unto thee shall surely die" (2 Samuel 12:13-14). David's response and subsequent repentance demonstrated the effectiveness of Nathan's sincere and brave confrontation. This story exemplifies several key aspects of biblical bravery and sincerity. First, it shows that bravery is not just about physical courage but also about moral courage—the willingness to stand up for what is right and to speak the truth, even to those in power. Nathan's confrontation of David required a deep commitment to God's truth and a willingness to risk his own well-being for the sake of righteousness. Second, it highlights the importance of sincerity in relationships and leadership. Nathan's approach was not manipulative or deceitful; it was straightforward and honest. He used a parable to help David see his own sin from a different perspective, but he did not shy away from delivering the direct and uncomfortable truth. Nathan's sincerity helped David to recognize the gravity of his actions and to repent, leading to his restoration and continued leadership. Third, the story underscores the power of repentance and forgiveness. David's acknowledgment of his sin and his sincere repentance opened the door for God's mercy. Despite the severe consequences of his actions, David's relationship with God was ultimately restored because he responded to Nathan's confrontation with humility and contrition. This narrative encourages believers to practice sincerity and bravery in their own lives. It challenges us to speak the truth in love, even when it is difficult or risky, and to hold ourselves and others accountable to God's standards. It also reminds us of the importance of repentance and the assurance of God's forgiveness when we turn back to Him with sincere hearts. In conclusion, Nathan's confrontation of David is a powerful example of biblical bravery and sincerity. Nathan's willingness to speak the truth to power, regardless of the potential consequences, demonstrates the moral courage that is at the heart of true bravery. His sincere approach helped to bring about David's repentance and restoration, highlighting the transformative power of truth and repentance. This story encourages believers to emulate Nathan's example by practicing sincerity and bravery in their own lives, speaking the truth in love, and seeking to uphold God's standards in all their interactions.

Chapter 6 – Service Of Biblical Bravery

"But a certain Samaritan, as he journeyed, came where he was: and when he saw him, he had compassion on him." (Luke 10:33)

In the Bible, the parable of the Good Samaritan is a profound example of service and bravery, illustrating how true bravery often involves compassionate action towards others, even when it is inconvenient or risky. This story, found in Luke 10:33, teaches us that bravery is not just about heroic deeds on the battlefield but also about everyday acts of kindness and service to those in need. The story begins with a lawyer asking Jesus a question to test Him: "Master, what shall I do to inherit eternal life?" Jesus responded by asking him what was written in the law. The lawyer answered, "Thou shalt love the Lord thy God with all thy heart, and with all thy soul, and with all thy strength, and with all thy mind; and thy neighbor as thyself." Jesus told him that he had answered correctly and that doing this would lead to life. However, seeking to justify himself, the lawyer asked Jesus, "And who is my neighbor?" In response, Jesus told the parable of the Good Samaritan.

In the parable, a man was traveling from Jerusalem to Jericho when he fell among thieves who stripped him of his clothes, wounded him, and left him half dead. A priest happened to be going down the same road, but when he saw the man, he passed by on the other side. Likewise, a Levite, when he came to the place and saw him, passed by on the other side. These two individuals, who were expected to show compassion and help, chose to ignore the man's plight and avoid getting involved.

Their actions reflected a lack of bravery and a failure to live out the principles of service and love that they were supposed to uphold.

Then came the Samaritan, a person who was generally despised by the Jews and considered an outsider. The Samaritan, as he journeyed, came to where the wounded man was. When he saw him, he had compassion on him. Despite the enmity between Jews and Samaritans and the potential danger of stopping on a road known for its hazards, the Samaritan did not hesitate. He went to the man, bound up his wounds, pouring on oil and wine. Then he set him on his own animal, brought him to an inn, and took care of him. The next day, he took out two denarii and gave them to the innkeeper, saying, "Take care of him; and whatsoever thou spendest more, when I come again, I will repay thee."

This act of kindness and bravery was remarkable because the Samaritan went out of his way to help someone who was considered his enemy. He risked his own safety, spent his own money, and took time from his journey to ensure the injured man received proper care. The Samaritan's actions demonstrate the essence of true service—selfless, compassionate, and courageous. He did not allow societal prejudices or personal risk to deter him from doing what was right. His bravery lay in his willingness to serve someone in need, regardless of the potential cost to himself.

After telling the parable, Jesus asked the lawyer, "Which now of these three, thinkest thou, was neighbor unto him that fell among the thieves?" The lawyer replied, "He that shewed mercy on him." Then Jesus said to him, "Go, and do thou likewise." Through this parable, Jesus taught that true bravery and service involve showing mercy and compassion to others, even when it is difficult or inconvenient. The Samaritan's actions are a powerful reminder that bravery is not just about grand gestures but also about the everyday choices we make to help those in need.

The parable of the Good Samaritan challenges us to reflect on our own lives and consider how we can be more like the Samaritan in our interactions with others. It calls us to act with compassion and courage, putting aside our biases and fears to serve those who are hurting. This kind of bravery is rooted in love and a commitment to doing what is right, regardless of the circumstances.

The story also highlights the importance of seeing everyone as our neighbor, deserving of our care and compassion. The priest and the Levite failed to see the wounded man as their neighbor, while the Samaritan saw beyond ethnic and cultural divisions to the common humanity they shared. This perspective is essential for fostering a more compassionate and just world.

Moreover, the Samaritan's example teaches us that true service requires personal sacrifice. He gave of his time, resources, and energy to help the wounded man, expecting nothing in return. This selflessness is at the heart of genuine service and bravery. It challenges us to be willing to make sacrifices for the well-being of others, even when it is not easy or convenient.

In conclusion, the parable of the Good Samaritan is a powerful illustration of biblical bravery and service. The Samaritan's willingness to help the injured man, despite the risks and societal prejudices, exemplifies the kind of bravery that Jesus calls us to embody. This story teaches us that true bravery involves compassionate action and selfless service to others, seeing everyone as our neighbor and being willing to make personal sacrifices for their well-being. The Good Samaritan's example encourages us to live out our faith through acts of kindness and service, demonstrating the love of God to a hurting world. By following the Samaritan's example, we can make a profound impact on the lives of others and fulfill the commandment to love our neighbors as ourselves.

Chapter 7 - Self-Control of Biblical Bravery

"But he refused, and said unto his master's wife, Behold, my master wotteth not what is with me in the house, and he hath committed all that he hath to my hand." (Genesis 39:8)

In the Bible, the story of Joseph resisting Potiphar's wife is a remarkable example of self-control and bravery, illustrating how true bravery involves making difficult but morally right choices, even in the face of persistent temptation and potential personal loss. This story, found in Genesis 39, highlights Joseph's unwavering commitment to integrity and faithfulness to God, even when he was far from home and facing relentless pressure. Joseph, sold into slavery by his jealous brothers, found himself in Egypt as a servant in the house of Potiphar, an officer of Pharaoh. Despite his circumstances, Joseph rose to a position of great responsibility due to his diligence and the favor of God, which was evident in everything he did. Potiphar trusted Joseph completely, placing him in charge of his entire household and all his possessions. However, Joseph's integrity and dedication were soon put to a severe test. Potiphar's wife took notice of Joseph, who was described as well-built and handsome, and began to seduce him. She repeatedly tried to entice him, saying, "Lie with me." This persistent temptation was not just a one-time occurrence but a continuous challenge that Joseph faced daily. Despite the repeated advances, Joseph consistently refused, demonstrating remarkable self-control and bravery.

Joseph's refusal was not merely an act of personal morality but a declaration of his loyalty to both his master and God. He said to Potiphar's wife, "Behold, my master wotteth not what is with me in the house, and he hath committed all that he hath to my hand; there is none greater in this house than I; neither hath he kept back any thing from me but thee, because thou art his wife: how then can I do this great wickedness, and sin against God?" (Genesis 39:8-9). This response underscores the depth of Joseph's integrity and his awareness of the trust placed in him by Potiphar. More importantly, it reflects his profound sense of accountability to God. For Joseph, the idea of betraying his master's trust and sinning against God was unthinkable, regardless of the temptation he faced. Joseph's resistance required continuous vigilance and strength of character. Potiphar's wife's advances were not a singular event but a persistent assault on his moral resolve. Day after day, she tried to wear him down, but Joseph's self-control and commitment to righteousness did not waver. This consistency in the face of temptation is a key aspect of his bravery. It's one thing to resist temptation once, but it requires extraordinary bravery and self-control to stand firm repeatedly, especially when the temptation is both persistent and enticing. The situation escalated when Potiphar's wife, frustrated by Joseph's steadfast refusals, decided to trap him. One day, when none of the household servants were inside, she caught him by his garment and said, "Lie with me." Joseph, realizing the gravity of the situation, fled from her presence, leaving his garment in her hand as he ran out of the house. This act of fleeing was both a physical and moral escape from sin. Joseph's decision to run, even though it meant leaving behind his garment and potentially facing false accusations, highlights his unwavering commitment to maintain his integrity and purity.

Potiphar's wife, scorned by Joseph's rejection, concocted a lie, accusing Joseph of attempting to assault her. She used the garment he left behind as false evidence to support her claim. When Potiphar returned home, she told him the fabricated story, saying that Joseph had come in to mock her and that she screamed, causing him to flee, leaving his garment behind. Potiphar, believing his wife's accusation, was furious and had Joseph thrown into prison. Despite being innocent, Joseph did not retaliate or seek revenge. Instead, he accepted the unjust punishment with grace, demonstrating remarkable bravery and trust in God's justice. Even in prison, Joseph's integrity and faithfulness continued to shine. The Lord was with him, and he found favor in the eyes of the prison warden, who put him in charge of all the prisoners and the prison's operations. Joseph's ability to maintain his faith and integrity in such adverse circumstances speaks volumes about his character. His self-control and bravery were not dependent on his external situation but were deeply rooted in his relationship with God and his commitment to righteousness.

The story of Joseph and Potiphar's wife offers several important lessons about self-control and bravery. First, it teaches that true bravery involves the strength to resist temptation, even when it is persistent and enticing. Joseph's repeated refusals in the face of daily temptation demonstrate that self-control is an ongoing battle that requires continuous vigilance and commitment. His bravery was not just in a single act of resistance but in his consistent ability to stand firm against repeated advances. Second, the story highlights the importance of integrity and faithfulness. Joseph's refusal to sin against his master and God, despite the potential personal cost, underscores the value of maintaining one's principles and integrity, even when no one else is watching. His loyalty to Potiphar and his accountability to God were paramount in his decision-making process, reflecting a deep sense of honor and righteousness.

Third, Joseph's willingness to flee from temptation, even at the cost of leaving behind his garment and facing false accusations, illustrates the principle that sometimes the bravest thing to do is to run from sin. This act of fleeing is not a sign of weakness but of strength and wisdom. Joseph recognized that staying in the situation could lead to greater temptation and chose to remove himself entirely, prioritizing his spiritual and moral integrity over his physical presence. Additionally, Joseph's response to the false accusations and his subsequent imprisonment teaches us about enduring unjust suffering with grace and faith. Despite being wrongfully accused and imprisoned, Joseph did not become bitter or seek revenge. Instead, he continued to trust in God's plan and remained faithful, even in the harsh conditions of prison. His ability to maintain his character and faith in the face of injustice is a testament to his extraordinary bravery and self-control.

Furthermore, the story of Joseph and Potiphar's wife demonstrates that God's presence and favor are not limited by our circumstances. Even in prison, God was with Joseph, granting him favor and success. This teaches us that maintaining our integrity and faithfulness, even in difficult and unjust situations, can lead to God's blessing and favor, regardless of our external circumstances. Joseph's story encourages us to trust in God's justice and timing, knowing that He sees our struggles and will ultimately vindicate us. In conclusion, the story of Joseph resisting Potiphar's wife is a powerful example of biblical bravery and self-control. Joseph's unwavering commitment to integrity and righteousness, his consistent resistance to persistent temptation, and his graceful endurance of unjust suffering highlight the essence of true bravery. His actions teach us that bravery involves the strength to stand firm in our principles, to flee from sin, and to trust in God's justice and timing. Joseph's example challenges us to practice self-control and integrity in our own lives, demonstrating that true bravery is rooted in our relationship with God and our commitment to His standards of righteousness. This story encourages us to emulate Joseph's example by resisting temptation, maintaining our integrity, and trusting in God's presence and favor, even in the face of adversity.

Chapter 8 – Spirituality of Biblical Bravery

"Now when Daniel knew that the writing was signed, he went into his house... and he kneeled upon his knees three times a day, and prayed..." (Daniel 6:10)

In the Bible, the story of Daniel and his unwavering prayer life is a powerful example of spiritual bravery. This story, found in Daniel 6:10, showcases Daniel's commitment to his faith and his courage in maintaining his spiritual practices despite facing life-threatening consequences. Daniel was a young man of noble birth who was taken captive by the Babylonians and brought to Babylon when he was still a teenager. Despite being in a foreign land with different customs and gods, Daniel remained faithful to the God of Israel. He quickly rose to a position of prominence due to his wisdom, integrity, and the favor of God, eventually becoming one of the top administrators under King Darius. Daniel's faithfulness and excellence, however, provoked jealousy among the other administrators and satraps. Seeking to find grounds for charges against Daniel in his conduct of government affairs, they could find no corruption in him, because he was trustworthy and neither corrupt nor negligent. Frustrated, they devised a plan to trap Daniel using his own religious practices. They approached King Darius and proposed a decree that anyone who prayed to any god or human being during the next thirty days, except to the king, should be thrown into the lions' den. The king, flattered by their suggestion and unaware of their malicious intent, signed the decree into law. The law of the

Medes and Persians, once signed, could not be altered or repealed.

Daniel, knowing that the decree had been published, faced a critical decision. He could have chosen to pray in secret to avoid detection or to cease his prayers altogether to save his life. However, Daniel's spirituality and his relationship with God were more important to him than his own safety. Demonstrating incredible bravery and unwavering faith, Daniel chose to continue his usual practice of praying three times a day, with his windows open toward Jerusalem. The Bible records, "Now when Daniel knew that the writing was signed, he went into his house; and his windows being open in his chamber toward Jerusalem, he kneeled upon his knees three times a day, and prayed, and gave thanks before his God, as he did aforetime" (Daniel 6:10). This act of bravery was not a one-time defiance but a continuation of his lifelong spiritual discipline. Daniel's decision to pray openly, knowing the consequences, highlights the depth of his faith and his courage. He understood the importance of maintaining his connection with God and did not allow fear or the threat of death to interfere with his spiritual practices. Daniel's unwavering prayer life demonstrates that true bravery is not just about physical courage but also about spiritual steadfastness. His actions teach us that maintaining our spiritual disciplines, even in the face of opposition or danger, is a form of bravery that honors God and strengthens our faith.

When Daniel's enemies discovered him praying and petitioning God, they immediately went to the king to report his disobedience. They reminded the king of the decree and the irrevocable nature of the law of the Medes and Persians. Although the king was greatly distressed and determined to rescue Daniel, he was bound by the law and had no choice but to order Daniel to be thrown into the lions' den. Before carrying out the sentence, the king said to Daniel, "Thy God whom thou servest continually, he will deliver thee" (Daniel 6:16). A stone was brought and placed over the mouth of the den, and the king sealed it with his own signet ring and with the rings of his nobles, so that Daniel's situation might not be changed. The king returned to his palace and spent the night without eating and without any entertainment being brought to him, and he could not sleep. At the first light of dawn, the king hurried to the lions' den. When he came near the den, he called to Daniel in an anguished voice, "O Daniel, servant of the living God, is thy God, whom thou servest continually, able to deliver thee from the lions?" (Daniel 6:20). Daniel answered, "O king, live for ever. My God hath sent his angel, and hath shut the lions' mouths, that they have not hurt me: forasmuch as before him innocency was found in me; and also before thee, O king, have I done no hurt" (Daniel 6:21-22). The king was overjoyed and gave orders to lift Daniel out of the den. When Daniel was lifted from the den, no wound was found on him because he had trusted in his God. The king then commanded that the men who had falsely accused Daniel be brought in and thrown into the lions' den, along with their wives and children. Before they reached the floor of the den, the lions overpowered them and crushed all their bones. King Darius then wrote to all the nations and peoples of every language in all the earth, "I make a decree, That in every dominion of my kingdom men tremble and fear before the God of Daniel: for he is the living God, and stedfast for ever, and his kingdom that which shall not be destroyed, and his dominion shall be even unto the end. He delivereth and rescueth, and he worketh signs and wonders in heaven and in earth, who hath delivered Daniel from the power of the lions" (Daniel 6:26-27).

The story of Daniel in the lions' den is a testament to the power of faith and the protection of God for those who remain steadfast in their spiritual practices. Daniel's unwavering commitment to prayer, even under the threat of death, exemplifies the kind of spiritual bravery that believers are called to exhibit. His actions demonstrate that true bravery involves prioritizing our relationship with God above all else and trusting in His power to deliver and protect us. Daniel's example also teaches us about the importance of consistency in our spiritual disciplines. His habit of praying three times a day was not something he did only in times of crisis but was a regular part of his daily life. This consistency in seeking God and maintaining his spiritual practices provided Daniel with the strength and courage to face the lions' den with faith and confidence. His story challenges us to develop and maintain our own spiritual disciplines, so that we too can stand firm in our faith, regardless of the circumstances we face.

Furthermore, Daniel's story highlights the impact that one person's faithfulness can have on others. The miraculous deliverance of Daniel from the lions' den led to King Darius acknowledging the power and sovereignty of the God of Israel and issuing a decree that all people in his kingdom should fear and reverence the God of Daniel. Daniel's bravery and faithfulness not only saved his life but also brought glory to God and influenced a pagan king and his entire kingdom. This underscores the idea that our spiritual bravery can have far-reaching effects, inspiring others to recognize and honor the true God.

In conclusion, Daniel's unwavering prayer life is a powerful example of biblical bravery. His commitment to maintaining his spiritual practices, even in the face of deadly consequences, exemplifies the essence of true spiritual bravery. Daniel's story teaches us that bravery involves prioritizing our relationship with God, being consistent in our spiritual disciplines, and trusting in God's power to deliver and protect us. It challenges us to develop our own spiritual bravery by remaining faithful and steadfast in our practices, regardless of the opposition or dangers we may face. Daniel's example encourages us to stand firm in our faith, knowing that our spiritual bravery can bring glory to God and positively impact those around us.

Chapter 9 – Solidarity of Biblical Bravery

"Go, gather together all the Jews that are present in Shushan, and fast ye for me... and so will I go in unto the king..." (Esther 4:16)

In the Bible, the story of Esther is a profound example of bravery rooted in solidarity, showcasing how courage and unity can bring about salvation and justice for a people facing annihilation. Esther, a Jewish woman who became queen of Persia, demonstrated remarkable bravery when she risked her life to plead for the safety of her people. This story, particularly highlighted in Esther 4:16, reveals the depth of her courage and the importance of solidarity in the face of immense danger. Esther's journey to bravery began when she was chosen to be queen by King Ahasuerus, also known as Xerxes. She kept her Jewish identity a secret on the advice of her cousin Mordecai, who had raised her. Everything changed when Haman, an advisor to the king, plotted to destroy all the Jews in the kingdom out of hatred for Mordecai, who refused to bow to him. Haman's plan was set into motion with the king's approval, and a decree was issued to annihilate the Jews on a specific date. When Mordecai learned of this plot, he tore his clothes, put on sackcloth and ashes, and went into the city, wailing loudly and bitterly. He then sent a message to Esther, urging her to go to the king and beg for mercy for her people. Esther was initially hesitant because approaching the king unsummoned could result in death, unless the king extended his golden scepter to her. This law applied to everyone, including the queen. Despite the grave risk, Mordecai's words spurred Esther into action. He reminded her that her position as queen did not exempt her from the fate of her people and that she might have been placed in her royal position "for such a time as this" (Esther 4:14).

Understanding the gravity of the situation, Esther's response was one of solidarity and bravery. She sent a reply to Mordecai: "Go, gather together all the Jews that are present in Shushan, and fast ye for me, and neither eat nor drink three days, night or day: I also and my maidens will fast likewise; and so will I go in unto the king, which is not according to the law: and if I perish, I perish" (Esther 4:16). This statement is a testament to her willingness to sacrifice her life for the sake of her people. Esther's request for fasting was a call for unity and collective prayer, demonstrating her reliance on God and the strength that comes from solidarity. The Jews of Susa heeded her call, joining together in a three-day fast. This act of collective prayer and fasting underscores the power of unity and spiritual solidarity in times of crisis. Esther's bravery was not just in her willingness to risk her life but also in her understanding that she needed the support and prayers of her community.

After the three days of fasting and prayer, Esther dressed in her royal robes and went to the inner court of the king's palace. As she stood before the king, he saw her and was pleased, extending his golden scepter to her, sparing her life. When the king asked what she desired, Esther invited him and Haman to a banquet she had prepared. At the banquet, the king again asked Esther what her request was, promising to grant it up to half his kingdom. Esther, displaying both wisdom and bravery, invited the king and Haman to another banquet the next day, where she would make her petition known. During this second banquet, Esther revealed her Jewish identity and exposed Haman's plot, saying, "If I have found favor in thy sight, O king, and if it please the king, let my life be given me at my petition, and my people at my request: For we are sold, I and my people, to be destroyed, to be slain, and to perish" (Esther 7:3-4). King Ahasuerus was enraged and demanded to know who was responsible for this plot. Esther pointed to Haman, saying, "The adversary and enemy is this wicked Haman" (Esther 7:6). The king, in his fury, had Haman hanged on the very gallows he had prepared for Mordecai.

However, the decree to annihilate the Jews was still in effect, as Persian laws could not be revoked. Esther once again approached the king, falling at his feet and weeping, begging him to put an end to Haman's evil plan. The king extended his scepter to her again, allowing her to rise and speak. Esther pleaded, "If it please the king, and if I have found favor in his sight, and the thing seem right before the king, and I be pleasing in his eyes, let it be written to reverse the letters devised by Haman... which he wrote to destroy the Jews which are in all the king's provinces" (Esther 8:5). King Ahasuerus then allowed Mordecai and Esther to write a new decree, granting the Jews the right to defend themselves against any attack. This new decree was sent out swiftly, and on the day that had been set for their destruction, the Jews were able to protect themselves, resulting in their victory over their enemies. The bravery of Esther, combined with the solidarity of the Jewish people, led to their deliverance.

Esther's story teaches several important lessons about bravery and solidarity. First, it shows that true bravery involves standing up for others, even at great personal risk. Esther could have remained silent and safe within the palace, but she chose to identify with her people and risk her life to save them. Her actions demonstrate that bravery is not just about personal courage but also about a deep commitment to justice and the well-being of others. Second, the story highlights the power of solidarity and collective action. Esther's call for fasting and prayer united the Jewish community, strengthening them spiritually and preparing them for the challenge ahead. This collective effort underscores the idea that bravery is often supported and amplified by the unity and prayers of others. The Jewish community's response to Esther's call for solidarity played a crucial role in their ultimate deliverance. Third, Esther's story emphasizes the importance of wisdom and strategic action in conjunction with bravery. Esther did not rush into the king's presence impulsively; she carefully planned her approach, using the banquets to build a favorable atmosphere before making her request. Her strategic thinking and patience were vital in ensuring the success of her plea.

Furthermore, Esther's story reveals the significance of identity and courage in the face of oppression. By revealing her Jewish identity to the king, Esther took a stand against the systemic discrimination and hatred orchestrated by Haman. Her bravery in declaring her identity and speaking out against injustice is a powerful reminder of the impact that one person's courage can have in confronting and dismantling systems of oppression. The story of Esther also highlights the role of divine providence in acts of bravery. Throughout the narrative, it is evident that God's hand was at work, guiding and protecting Esther and her people. Her bravery and the solidarity of the Jewish community were complemented by God's favor and intervention, leading to their deliverance. This underscores the idea that acts of bravery, especially those rooted in faith and solidarity, are often supported by divine providence.

In conclusion, the story of Esther's plea for her people is a powerful example of biblical bravery and solidarity. Esther's willingness to risk her life for the sake of her people, her strategic approach to petitioning the king, and the united prayer and fasting of the Jewish community demonstrate the profound impact of bravery and solidarity in the face of injustice. Her story teaches us that true bravery involves standing up for others, even at great personal risk, and that such acts of courage are often supported by the unity and prayers of others. Esther's example challenges us to consider how we can stand in solidarity with those who are oppressed and to use our voices and actions to bring about justice and deliverance. Her story encourages us to trust in divine providence and to believe that our acts of bravery and solidarity can lead to significant and positive change in the world.

Chapter 10 – Stamina of Biblical Bravery

"Are they ministers of Christ?... in labours more abundant, in stripes above measure, in prisons more frequent, in deaths oft." (2 Corinthians 11:23)

In the Bible, the story of Paul and his missionary journeys is a profound example of stamina and biblical bravery, showcasing the relentless commitment and perseverance required to spread the gospel despite facing immense hardships and dangers. Paul's life, as detailed in the New Testament, particularly in his own words in 2 Corinthians 11:23, highlights the extraordinary endurance and courage needed to fulfill his mission. Paul's journeys took him across vast regions, preaching the message of Jesus Christ to Jews and Gentiles alike. His unwavering dedication to his calling, despite the constant threat of persecution, physical suffering, and even death, is a testament to his remarkable stamina and spiritual bravery.

Paul's missionary work began after his dramatic conversion on the road to Damascus. Initially a fervent persecutor of Christians, Paul encountered Jesus in a vision that transformed him into one of the most devoted apostles. This transformation marked the beginning of a life filled with tireless evangelism. Paul undertook multiple missionary journeys, traveling thousands of miles by land and sea, establishing churches, and nurturing fledgling Christian communities. His travels took him through regions such as Asia Minor, Macedonia, Greece, and Rome. These journeys were fraught with challenges, including opposition from both Jewish and Roman authorities, as well as from local populations who were hostile to his message.

In his letter to the Corinthians, Paul recounts the extent of his suffering, saying, "Are they ministers of Christ? (I speak as a fool) I am more; in labours more abundant, in stripes above measure, in prisons more frequent, in deaths oft." (2 Corinthians 11:23). He elaborates on his hardships, detailing how he was beaten with rods, stoned, shipwrecked, and constantly in danger from rivers, bandits, his own countrymen, and Gentiles. He experienced sleepless nights, hunger, thirst, cold, and exposure. Despite these relentless trials, Paul's stamina did not waver. His bravery was not merely in enduring physical suffering but in his steadfast commitment to his mission and his unshakeable faith in God's purpose for his life.

One notable example of Paul's stamina and bravery is his first missionary journey with Barnabas. They traveled to Cyprus and then to the region of Galatia, where they preached in cities like Iconium, Lystra, and Derbe. In Lystra, Paul was stoned by a hostile crowd and left for dead. Yet, displaying remarkable resilience, he got up and went back into the city the next day, continuing his mission. This incident is a powerful testament to his unwavering commitment and stamina. Paul's second missionary journey further exemplifies his stamina. Traveling with Silas, he ventured into Europe for the first time, establishing churches in Philippi, Thessalonica, and Corinth. In Philippi, Paul and Silas were severely beaten and imprisoned for casting out a spirit from a slave girl, an act that disrupted the local economy. While in prison, they prayed and sang hymns to God, and a miraculous earthquake opened the prison doors. Instead of escaping, Paul and Silas stayed and converted the jailer and his family to Christianity, demonstrating their dedication to spreading the gospel even in dire circumstances.

Paul's third missionary journey involved further travel and teaching, strengthening the churches he had previously founded. His time in Ephesus was marked by significant opposition from those who profited from the worship of the goddess Artemis. A riot ensued, endangering Paul's life, yet he continued to preach and teach boldly. Throughout his journeys, Paul also faced significant personal challenges, including what he referred to as a "thorn in the flesh," a persistent affliction that he endured with grace, relying on God's strength. Paul's final journey to Rome, where he was eventually martyred, further illustrates his stamina and bravery. Despite knowing the dangers awaiting him, Paul remained resolute in his mission. On his way to Rome, he survived a shipwreck and continued to preach the gospel even while under house arrest.

Paul's letters to the various churches he established reflect his deep concern for their spiritual well-being and his unwavering commitment to their growth in faith. He provided guidance, correction, encouragement, and doctrinal teaching, often writing these letters from prison. His epistles, such as Romans, Corinthians, Galatians, Ephesians, Philippians, Colossians, and Thessalonians, continue to inspire and instruct Christians around the world. Paul's stamina was fueled by his profound faith and the conviction that he was fulfilling God's purpose. He viewed his sufferings as part of his service to Christ, often expressing joy in his trials because they advanced the gospel. He wrote to the Philippians, "I can do all things through Christ which strengtheneth me" (Philippians 4:13), and to the Corinthians, he emphasized that his strength came from God, saying, "My grace is sufficient for thee: for my strength is made perfect in weakness" (2 Corinthians 12:9).

Paul's story teaches us that true bravery involves enduring hardships with unwavering faith and perseverance. His example challenges believers to remain steadfast in their faith and mission, regardless of the obstacles they may face. Paul's life is a testament to the power of divine strength and the importance of stamina in fulfilling one's calling. His missionary journeys, filled with peril and suffering, were marked by a relentless pursuit of spreading the gospel and nurturing the early Christian church. Through his example, we learn that spiritual stamina is not about avoiding difficulties but about facing them head-on with courage and faith in God's provision and purpose.

In conclusion, Paul's missionary journeys are a powerful example of biblical bravery and stamina. His relentless commitment to spreading the gospel, despite facing numerous hardships and dangers, exemplifies the essence of true bravery. Paul's endurance and unwavering faith in the face of persecution, physical suffering, and constant danger highlight the importance of stamina in fulfilling one's divine calling. His life teaches us that true bravery is rooted in steadfast faith, perseverance, and the unwavering pursuit of God's mission, regardless of the challenges we encounter. Paul's story encourages believers to remain committed to their faith and mission, trusting in God's strength and provision to sustain them through all trials.

Chapter 11 – Sensitivity of Biblical Bravery

"And Ruth said, Intreat me not to leave thee... for whither thou goest, I will go; and where thou lodgest, I will lodge..." (Ruth 1:16)

In the Bible, the story of Ruth and her unwavering loyalty to Naomi is a profound example of sensitivity and bravery, highlighting how true bravery often involves deep empathy, commitment, and selfless actions toward others in their times of need. This story, found in the Book of Ruth, particularly in Ruth 1:16, showcases Ruth's extraordinary sensitivity to Naomi's plight and her courageous decision to support her mother-in-law despite facing an uncertain and potentially harsh future. Ruth, a Moabite woman, was married to one of Naomi's sons. Tragedy struck when Naomi's husband and her two sons died, leaving Naomi and her two daughters-in-law, Ruth and Orpah, in a vulnerable position. Naomi decided to return to her homeland of Bethlehem after hearing that the Lord had provided food for His people there. She urged her daughters-in-law to return to their own mothers' homes, hoping they would find new husbands and have a better life in Moab. Orpah reluctantly agreed and returned to her people, but Ruth clung to Naomi, displaying remarkable sensitivity and bravery.

Ruth's response to Naomi's plea was filled with heartfelt determination and loyalty. She said, "Intreat me not to leave thee, or to return from following after thee: for whither thou goest, I will go; and where thou lodgest, I will lodge: thy people shall be my people, and thy God my God: Where thou diest, will

I die, and there will I be buried: the Lord do so to me, and more also, if ought but death part thee and me" (Ruth 1:16-17). This declaration is one of the most moving expressions of loyalty and bravery in the Bible. Ruth chose to leave her homeland, her people, and her gods to accompany Naomi to a foreign land, fully aware of the difficulties they might face. Her decision was driven by deep sensitivity to Naomi's suffering and a selfless desire to support her mother-in-law in her time of need. Ruth's bravery is evident in her willingness to embrace an uncertain future and endure potential hardships for the sake of loyalty and love.

When Ruth and Naomi arrived in Bethlehem, their situation was precarious. As widows without a male protector, they faced significant social and economic challenges. Ruth, however, did not hesitate to take on the role of provider. She displayed further bravery by going to the fields to glean grain, a practice allowed for the poor and the foreigner, to gather food for herself and Naomi. Ruth's initiative and hard work in the fields caught the attention of Boaz, a wealthy relative of Naomi's late husband. Boaz, impressed by Ruth's loyalty to Naomi and her diligent work, showed her kindness and protection, ensuring she had enough grain to gather and eat. He instructed his workers to leave extra grain for her to collect and invited her to eat with them, providing her with sustenance and security.

Ruth's sensitivity and bravery not only ensured the survival of herself and Naomi but also set the stage for God's greater plan. Boaz, recognizing Ruth's noble character and her loyalty to Naomi, took on the role of kinsman-redeemer, marrying Ruth and securing a future for her and Naomi. This marriage was significant, as it ensured the continuation of Naomi's family line and restored their social and economic status. Through their union, Ruth and Boaz became the great-grandparents of King David, placing Ruth in the direct lineage of Jesus Christ. This remarkable outcome highlights how acts of bravery and sensitivity, even in the face of great personal risk, can have profound and far-reaching implications.

Ruth's story teaches several important lessons about bravery and sensitivity. First, it shows that true bravery is not just about physical courage but also about emotional strength and the willingness to support others in their time of need. Ruth's sensitivity to Naomi's suffering and her selfless decision to stay with her mother-in-law, despite the potential hardships, exemplify the essence of true bravery. Her actions demonstrate that sensitivity and empathy are powerful motivators for courageous and selfless acts.

Second, Ruth's story highlights the importance of loyalty and commitment. Ruth's unwavering loyalty to Naomi, even when it meant leaving behind her own family and homeland, underscores the value of steadfast commitment to those we care about. Her bravery was rooted in her deep sense of duty and love for Naomi, showing that true loyalty often involves making significant sacrifices for the well-being of others.

Third, Ruth's story emphasizes the importance of taking initiative and working hard, even in difficult circumstances. Ruth did not passively wait for help but actively sought ways to provide for herself and Naomi by gleaning in the fields. Her diligence and determination were crucial in securing their survival and eventual redemption. This aspect of her bravery teaches us the value of proactive efforts and perseverance in the face of adversity.

Furthermore, Ruth's story highlights the power of God's providence and the interconnectedness of our actions within His greater plan. Ruth's bravery and sensitivity not only provided immediate relief for herself and Naomi but also played a pivotal role in God's redemptive plan for Israel. Her inclusion in the lineage of David and Jesus Christ demonstrates how acts of bravery and faithfulness can have a lasting and transformative impact on the course of history.

In conclusion, the story of Ruth's loyalty to Naomi is a powerful example of biblical bravery rooted in sensitivity. Ruth's decision to stay with Naomi, despite the uncertainties and potential hardships, showcases her extraordinary empathy, loyalty, and courage. Her actions demonstrate that true bravery involves emotional strength, a deep sense of duty, and a willingness to support others selflessly. Ruth's story challenges us to consider how we can exhibit similar sensitivity and bravery in our own lives, supporting those in need with empathy and commitment. Her example encourages us to embrace loyalty, take initiative, and trust in God's providence, knowing that our acts of bravery and sensitivity can have profound and far-reaching effects.

Chapter 12 – Solitude in Biblical Bravery

"And he came thither unto a cave, and lodged there; and, behold, the word of the Lord came to him, and he said unto him, What doest thou here, Elijah?" (1 Kings 19:9)

In the Bible, the story of Elijah at Mount Horeb is a profound example of bravery in solitude, highlighting how true bravery can involve facing one's deepest fears and doubts alone, while seeking and trusting in God's presence and guidance. This story, found in 1 Kings 19:9, showcases the prophet Elijah's journey through despair, loneliness, and divine encounter, revealing the spiritual strength and courage required to confront such personal challenges. Elijah, a mighty prophet of God, had just experienced a tremendous victory on Mount Carmel, where he defeated the prophets of Baal by calling down fire from heaven to consume his offering, proving the power of the true God to the people of Israel. However, this triumph was quickly overshadowed by a threat from Queen Jezebel, who vowed to kill him in retaliation for the death of her prophets. Terrified and exhausted, Elijah fled for his life, traveling into the wilderness and eventually reaching Beersheba in Judah. There, he left his servant and continued alone into the desert, where he collapsed under a broom bush and prayed to die, saying, "It is enough; now, O Lord, take away my life; for I am not better than my fathers" (1 Kings 19:4). This moment of despair reflects the depth of Elijah's emotional and spiritual exhaustion, as he felt overwhelmed by the seemingly insurmountable challenges he faced and the apparent lack of lasting change in Israel despite his efforts.

In his solitude, Elijah fell asleep under the bush, but an angel of the Lord touched him and provided him with food and water, urging him to eat and drink, for the journey ahead was too much for him. Strengthened by this divine provision, Elijah traveled for forty days and forty nights until he reached Mount Horeb, also known as Mount Sinai, the mountain of God. There, he entered a cave and spent the night. It was in this cave, in the depth of his solitude, that the word of the Lord came to him, asking, "What doest thou here, Elijah?" (1 Kings 19:9). This question was not just about Elijah's physical location but also about his spiritual and emotional state. God's inquiry invited Elijah to express his fears, frustrations, and sense of isolation. Elijah poured out his heart, saying, "I have been very jealous for the Lord God of hosts: for the children of Israel have forsaken thy covenant, thrown down thine altars, and slain thy prophets with the sword; and I, even I only, am left; and they seek my life, to take it away" (1 Kings 19:10). His response reveals his profound sense of isolation and discouragement, believing that he was the only faithful prophet left and that his mission had ultimately failed.

God's response to Elijah's lament was both gentle and powerful. He instructed Elijah to stand on the mountain in the presence of the Lord, for the Lord was about to pass by. A great and powerful wind tore through the mountains, shattering rocks, but the Lord was not in the wind. After the wind, there was an earthquake, but the Lord was not in the earthquake. After the earthquake, a fire, but the Lord was not in the fire. And after the fire came a still small voice, a gentle whisper. When Elijah heard it, he pulled his cloak over his face and went out and stood at the entrance of the cave. Again, the voice asked, "What doest thou here, Elijah?" (1 Kings 19:13). Elijah repeated his earlier lament, and God, in His compassion, provided Elijah with a new direction and purpose. He instructed Elijah to return the way he came and go to the Desert of Damascus, where he was to anoint Hazael king over Aram, Jehu king over Israel, and Elisha to succeed him as prophet. God reassured Elijah that he was not alone, revealing that He had reserved seven thousand in Israel who had not bowed to Baal or kissed him.

This encounter at Mount Horeb illustrates several key aspects of biblical bravery in solitude. First, it shows that true bravery involves confronting our deepest fears and feelings of isolation head-on, even when it means facing them alone. Elijah's journey to Mount Horeb and his time in the cave represent his willingness to seek God in the midst of his despair and loneliness, trusting that God would meet him there. This kind of bravery requires a deep faith and a willingness to be vulnerable before God, expressing our true feelings and struggles. Second, Elijah's experience highlights the importance of listening for God's voice in the quiet moments of solitude. The still small voice that spoke to Elijah demonstrates that God often reveals Himself in gentle, subtle ways rather than through dramatic, overwhelming events. Elijah's ability to recognize and respond to this quiet whisper reflects his deep spiritual sensitivity and his bravery in waiting for God's guidance in the midst of his turmoil.

Third, God's provision for Elijah through the angel's care and His reassurances at Mount Horeb underscore the idea that even in our most solitary moments, we are not truly alone. God's presence and care are constant, providing strength and direction when we need it most. Elijah's experience reminds us that true bravery includes relying on God's provision and trusting in His presence, even when we feel isolated and overwhelmed. Additionally, Elijah's story emphasizes the importance of renewed purpose and direction in overcoming feelings of despair and isolation. God's instructions to Elijah to anoint new leaders and to mentor Elisha provided him with a renewed sense of mission and connection to others. This new direction not only affirmed Elijah's role as a prophet but also connected him with a community of faithful individuals, countering his sense of isolation.

Elijah's journey to Mount Horeb and his encounter with God in the cave serve as a powerful reminder that bravery in solitude involves seeking God's presence, listening for His guidance, and finding renewed purpose in His plans. It teaches us that even in our darkest moments of loneliness and despair, God is there, ready to provide the strength and direction we need to continue our journey. In conclusion, the story of Elijah at Mount Horeb is a profound example of biblical bravery in solitude. Elijah's willingness to confront his fears and seek God in his deepest despair showcases the spiritual strength required to navigate such challenges. His encounter with God on the mountain highlights the importance of listening for God's voice in the quiet moments and trusting in His presence and provision. Elijah's renewed purpose and direction emphasize the value of finding new meaning and connection in God's plans. This story encourages us to embrace solitude as an opportunity for spiritual growth and to trust that God's presence and guidance will sustain us through our most challenging times. Elijah's example teaches us that true bravery involves seeking

God in our solitude, listening for His gentle whisper, and finding strength and purpose in His presence, even when we feel alone.

Conclusion

As we conclude our exploration of "Biblical Bravery," it's important to reflect on the powerful lessons we've learned from the various stories and teachings within the Bible. Biblical bravery is not just about heroic acts; it's a deep-seated faith, unwavering moral integrity, and the courage to stand up for what is right, even in the face of adversity. This kind of bravery is exemplified by numerous biblical figures whose lives and actions provide timeless inspiration and guidance for us today.

Throughout the Bible, we see that true bravery starts with a profound faith in God. David's confrontation with Goliath, for instance, wasn't just a display of physical courage but an act of unwavering faith. David's belief in God's power and protection was the source of his bravery. This teaches us that our own courage must be rooted in a strong faith in God, trusting that He will guide and support us through life's challenges.

Moral integrity is another critical aspect of biblical bravery. Joseph's story, especially his resistance to Potiphar's wife's advances, highlights the importance of staying true to one's principles. Despite the potential consequences, Joseph chose to do what was right, demonstrating that bravery often involves making difficult ethical decisions. In our own lives, maintaining moral integrity, even when it's unpopular or risky, is a true act of bravery.

The willingness to act courageously in the face of danger is also a hallmark of biblical bravery. Esther's bravery in approaching the king to save her people is a profound example of this. Her famous words, "If I perish, I perish," show her readiness to sacrifice her safety for a greater good. This kind of bravery teaches us that sometimes we must take significant risks to help others and fulfill our God-given purposes.

Solidarity and support for others are essential components of biblical bravery. Ruth's loyalty to Naomi, choosing to stay with her and support her despite an uncertain future, exemplifies this. Her bravery was in her selfless commitment to Naomi's well-being. This reminds us that standing with and supporting others in their time of need is a powerful expression of bravery.

Endurance and perseverance in the face of trials are crucial elements of biblical bravery. The apostle Paul's relentless mission to spread the gospel, despite facing beatings, imprisonment, and other hardships, is a testament to his steadfast courage. His bravery came from his unwavering dedication to his calling. This teaches us that true bravery includes the strength to persist and remain faithful, even when we face significant challenges.

Forgiveness and reconciliation are also acts of bravery highlighted in the Bible. Joseph's forgiveness of his brothers, who sold him into slavery, shows the deep courage required to let go of bitterness and seek peace. In our own lives, choosing to forgive those who have wronged us and working towards reconciliation can be one of the bravest things we do.

In today's world, the lessons of biblical bravery are more relevant than ever. We are called to demonstrate faith, integrity, courage, support for others, perseverance, and forgiveness in our daily lives. By embodying these principles, we can navigate the complexities and challenges of modern life with the same kind of bravery shown by the heroes and heroines of the Bible.

As we go forward, let us draw strength and inspiration from these biblical examples. Whether we are facing personal trials, standing up for what is right, or helping others in need, we can rely on our faith in God to give us the courage to act bravely. By living out these principles of biblical bravery, we can make a positive impact on our world and fulfill the purposes God has for each of us.

Don't miss out!

Visit the website below and you can sign up to receive emails whenever Joshua Rhoades publishes a new book. There's no charge and no obligation.

https://books2read.com/r/B-A-AJLBB-HILWE

BOOKS 2 READ

Connecting independent readers to independent writers.

Did you love *Biblical Bravery*? Then you should read *Flee Fornication: The Plea For Purity*[1] by Joshua Rhoades!

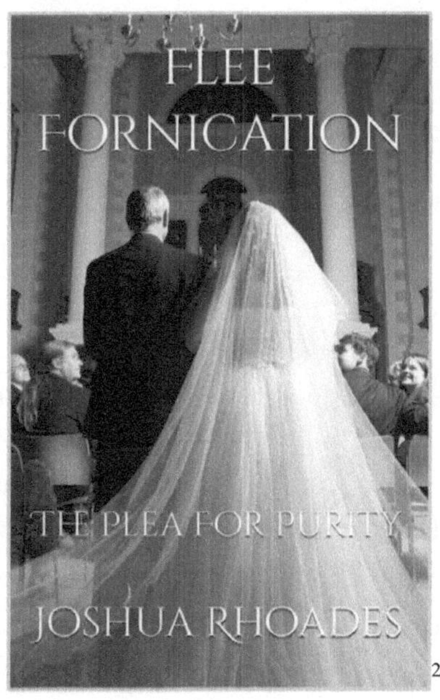

[2]

"Flee Fornication - The Plea For Purity" is an essential read for anyone grappling with the challenges of maintaining sexual purity in a world that often glorifies the opposite. This book dives deep into the spiritual and moral pitfalls that can ensnare individuals, drawing them away from a life of purity and toward a path of destruction. It doesn't shy away from addressing the real temptations and struggles that believers face daily, offering a candid look at the consequences of fornication, both spiritually and physically. Grounded in Scripture, calls readers to heed the

---

1. https://books2read.com/u/3GLqln

2. https://books2read.com/u/3GLqln

biblical plea found in 1 Corinthians 6:18, where the Apostle Paul urges, "Flee fornication. Every sin that a man doeth is without the body; but he that committeth fornication sinneth against his own body." This verse serves as the cornerstone of the book, emphasizing the severe spiritual implications of sexual immorality. From the story of Joseph fleeing Potiphar's wife to David's tragic fall with Bathsheba, the book illustrates the importance of vigilance and the devastating consequences of yielding to temptation. It also highlights the power of God's grace and the importance of repentance and restoration for those who have stumbled. The book doesn't just focus on the negative aspects but also provides uplifting encouragement on how to live a life of purity, including practical steps such as setting boundaries, avoiding compromising situations, and seeking accountability. The author stresses that purity is not just about saying "no" to sin but about saying "yes" to a deeper relationship with God. By committing to purity, believers can experience a closer walk with God, free from the guilt and shame that sexual sin brings. The book also considers the role of the Holy Spirit in empowering believers to overcome temptation and live a life that honors God. It is a call to action for those who desire to live a life that reflects the holiness of God, reminding readers that their bodies are temples of the Holy Spirit, and they are called to honor God with their bodies (1 Corinthians 6:19-20). "Flee Fornication - The Plea For Purity" is a powerful and timely message for a generation bombarded with sexual temptation, offering hope, healing, and a path to victory through Christ.